We Don't Need No Stinkin' Agent!

How To Sell Your Home Without Using One Of Those Pesky Real Estate Agents

We Don't Need No Stinkin' Agent!

How To Sell Your Home Without Using One Of Those Pesky Real Estate Agents

Jim Meyer

Jim Meyer
2019

First Printing: 2019

ISBN 978-0-359-670000

Jim Meyer
1411 Oliver Rd, Street # 180
Fairfield, California 94534

www.facebook.com/JamesEricMeyer

Table of Contents

Foreword

First off, thank you very much for reading this book. My intention for writing this book is to educate you as a homeowner on how to sell your own home.

Chances are you may have purchased your home without using an agent and you may have sold multiple homes without an agent.

Or maybe you are attempting to sell on your own for the very first time.

My goal is not to cover every single thing that could happen during the transaction or to predict everything that can go right or wrong. But I'd like to do my best to impart a little wisdom from my 20 + years of experience as a licensed real estate agent.

This being a fairly short book, you can easily read it in a very short time. Half of what you read, you may already be aware of, but I will guess that if you read every word, at least one paragraph may help you with your goal of selling your home for top dollar to a buyer who will not come back to sue you in the future.

Please, realize that I work in Northern California. If you live outside of California or even in the Central Valley or Southern California, things will operate a little differently. Always double check things I tell you with someone who has local expertise, like your neighbors, friends, and family who may have sold a home recently.

After you read the book for the first time, then you might want to hold onto it and use it as a checklist.

Included you will also find advice on how to talk to those agents who call and interrupt your day when your expectation is to get a call from a qualified buyer.

Thanks again for reading this book. Feel free to contact me anytime with suggestions for improving it on the next printing.

If you would like a digital version sent to you or a friend, please let me know.

If you would like another hard copy, contact me at any time.

Jim Meyer
Broker associate
RE/MAX Gold
License # 01036142
MeyerJames@Aol.Com
707-580-5391

Introduction

This book was written for you, the homeowner, whether you are using an agent or doing it yourself.

If you are using an agent now, you can still study my ideas and compare them to what your agent is doing?

The book is divided into two parts. Part 1 deals with why you may want to sell on your own, what to expect and how to manage the process? While Part 2 deals with what I think you should do if you decide that selling on your own is really not for you?

Finally, I included a glossary section of real estate terms in this book. Often times I talk to clients, just assuming they know more than they do. This can be a big mistake on my part. Throughout the entire process, I am constantly explaining things like escrow, contingencies, move out the date, final walk through, etc.

If you are doing this on your own, it can be a bit daunting not to have someone to talk to. Hopefully, this book will make it a little easier for you.

First off, who am I? My name is James (Jim) Meyer. I am a licensed broker associate with RE/MAX Gold. RE/MAX Gold has 60 + offices all over California.

For 20 + years, I have been a full-time Realtor®. Having started out with 21st Century in the late 1990s, I later moved to RE/MAX and now have my team, the "Meyer Team."

Thanks to a debilitating disease; walking is very difficult and going upstairs is pretty much impossible for me. Fortunately, my awesome team makes serving our clients a breeze as I work from my home office and they go out in the field. The set-up we have; is extremely efficient and my little problem may be a blessing as our clients get top-notch service from people who meet them in person, show them properties, get inspections done, etc. While, I used to handle things from my phone and computer.

But enough about me, let's go over how to sell your home ASAP for top dollar.

Section 1: Why You Should Not Use An Agent

Chapter 1: Ten Reasons Why You Should Not Use Real Estate Agents

#1 Depending on the sales price of your home, an agent will probably be making $100 per hour serving you. If you learn everything you need to learn, you can pocket that money and end up saving thousands; if not tens of thousands of dollars. Why not study a little and save a lot?

#2 You are a better negotiator than most agents. Since it is your home, you benefit a lot more than any real estate agent when your home sells for top dollar, so why allow some amateur the opportunity to negotiate on your behalf when you have been buying and selling cars, homes, cameras and baseball cards since before most agents go their license?

#3 Agents are greedy. The real estate agent who drives up in the fancy car that costs more than most people make in a year is primarily looking out for themselves, their next car payment and how they are going to pay for the next big vacation? There is no reason for you to pay for their next German luxury car. It's time to save some money for your kid's college fund.

#4 Agents disappear the minute you sign the listing agreement. You want to work with someone who will be available almost 24/7 for you, especially if you have not done this before. Since many agents promise the world and go to Hawaii the minute the sign goes up in your yard, you might as well do it all yourself.

#5 Because most buyers find the home they want through the internet or the sign in the front yard, why on Earth would you need Joe Agent with his clever "marketing skills?" You know how to put up a sign and you can easily market your home for sale much more inexpensively than that with Joe Agent!

#6 Any idiot can hold an open house. Getting a few open house signs, strategically placing starting five blocks away and leading people to your home is not rocket science. An agent can bake some cookies, turn on some soft music and hand out flyers for 6 % or you can do it yourself. You could also hire your high school son or daughter to help you out.

#7 They lie! Agents will tell you that you can't get your home listed on the MLS without thcm. Well, that is not true. There are brokers who will charge you a nominal fee; so that you can put your home on the MLS at a fraction of that commission cost.

#8 Another misnomer is that you can't get help from an agent if you do not sign a listing. Not true at all. You can easily offer a smaller than 6 % commission (like 3 %) to an agent who brings in a buyer. This agent will give you all the mandatory disclosures that you need.

#9 Agents can complicate things with all their going back and forth, dickering on the price and talking about who gets custody of the refrigerator, washer, and dryer etc. You get along well with people. All you need to do is sit down at the dining room table and hash out everything that the buyer wants and that you want. Within an hour or less, you can come up with a compromise that makes everyone happy instead of signing a counteroffer that your agent fills out for you, sending that to another agent who represents the buyer and then waiting 24 hours for a counter to your counteroffer to come through. In the time it takes to do all of that, you could have been doing a hundred other more important things with your life.

10 Finally, real estate agents are just obsolete. You can order prescription glasses online, you can order something from Amazon ® and get it in a day, you can get approved for a loan in a few hours, so why do real estate agents think they are still relevant? If you study this book, you should be on your way to cutting out the middleman or woman!

Chapter 2: How To Price Your Home

You decided that you want to sell your home yourself and you have a pretty good idea of what you want for your home, but you just are not sure.

If you go to popular sites like Zillow ® or Trulia ®, you will find value estimates that are not often very accurate.

These sites pull up information like square footage, the number of bedrooms, baths, proximity to your home and they come up with a number.

The sites have no way of knowing that you just replaced your roof and remodeled the kitchen.

One way to get good comparable sales is to contact your local title or escrow company. They can get you a property profile along with sold comps.

You can easily get active comps by going online and searching for your neighborhood. It's good to sign up with the major sites to get an email notification whenever a new listing comes on the market in the area.

You should also go to any and all open houses in the area. with this way, you will gain first-hand knowledge about the condition of the competition.

When you talk to the rep at the escrow company, you can also ask for a seller's net sheet.

This is vitally important for when you start negotiating the price.

You should tell the escrow officer about how much you want to sell your house for? You will tell them roughly what your loan payoff is? You can even give your loan # and last four digits of your social security number and the escrow officer should be willing to call the lender for a pay-off demand.

For the seller net sheet, you want to decide if you want the buyer to pay for a home warranty and if you are going to pay for, or ask the buyers to pay for, or split title and escrow fees.

As far as the warranty is concerned, it is a very good idea to make sure the buyer gets a home warranty.

If you pay for it, or the buyer pays for it or if the buyer brings in an agent and they pay for it; it is pretty smart for you to make sure that there is a 12-month home warranty in place.

The reason for making sure the buyer gets the warranty is simple. Something most likely is going to go wrong right after you close escrow. Even though you sold your home as is, the water heater could blow up the day the buyers move in. The buyers loved you yesterday and today they think you knew all about the water heater and they insist that you pay for it even though you disclosed that it was twenty years old and an inspector suggested the buyer get it replaced. All that buyer thinks right now is that they were ripped off.

With a warranty, the buyer simply pays a fee for a service call and the water heater is replaced and you never hear about it.

I mention water heaters because I just received an email from a warranty company detailing more than $2,000 that had been spent on repairs on one particular property that I sold last year.

On the net sheet, you will have transfer taxes. Where I am? Most cities in my county do not have a city transfer tax, but there is a county transfer tax in most, if not all counties.

Your escrow officer will know if you have to pay a city transfer tax and they can calculate it in their net sheet. The officer can tell you about what the custom is as far as who pays what expenses in your area? You can also go online and get this information. You can get the seller net sheet online too at most if not all the local title or escrow company websites.

Personally, I like contacting my local escrow officer to help me with this; so that the net sheet will be more accurate. They can also look up to see if there are unpaid taxes or city liens like garbage bills that need to be paid.

It's good to use an escrow officer who is local. There is also a chance that you are selling a mobile home. These are different than regular "stick built homes" especially if they are in a park. Over the years, I have sold quite a few mobile homes and it is important to work with a title company and escrow officer who knows how to handle these transactions?

You also may not have lived in the home for 2 years as your primary residence or maybe the home is an investment. Make sure that you tell the escrow officer on day one; so that they can tell you if maybe they have to hold a percentage of the proceeds to go to the state government.

As far as paying capital gains tax, please talk to an accountant and make sure you know if you are liable for any such tax before you put that "for sale sign" up.

There are other expenses that will go on the seller's net sheet. Ensure that you and the escrow officer should go over the details. Of course, you are planning on NOT PAYING a 6 % commission! But you may offer a buyer's agent a 3 % commission for bringing you the buyer. Don't forget to factor that in.

In case you do not know it, commissions are negotiable and don't let anyone tell you that 6 % is the standard commission and no one pays less. A seller of a $30,000 studio condo may pay more than 8 % and the seller of a ten-million-dollar mansion will probably pay 5 %.

If you work with the same agent, again and again, then I'd think they'd be happy to give you a break.

So, now you have done your research and you have an idea of how much is your home's worth?

You have a seller's net sheet that shows how much you will put in your pocket after the close of escrow and you feel pretty confident that your home is worth $550,000.

The big question is, do you ask more than $ 550,000, expecting to negotiate down? Or do you ask less, expecting the price to be bid upward?

Realize this: Most people are searching for homes on the internet or they have someone (an agent) searching for them. There are a lot more people doing searches up to $550,000 than up to $575,000.

So, if you think you will "test the waters" at $ 575,000, you could be listening to the crickets for two or three weeks before you get the idea to lower the price.

If you start at $549,000, you will get all the buyers who are searching up to $600,000 most likely. Therefore, pricing your home a little lower than higher can be a profitable practice.

The only time it can be a mistake is if you accept the first offer that comes along. It's always a good idea to list your home for sale early in the week, do not show it until the open house that weekend and then review and respond to offers right before the second weekend.

If you can't negotiate a good deal for yourself, then you should have open house # 2.

If you see yourself heading toward open house # 3, then there probably is a problem.

Some problems can be graduations, holidays, severe weather or rising interest rates. But most often the real problem is that you are asking too much for your home.

It's good to lower the price before your home becomes a "dead listing."

When people search for your home online, they will see how many days it has been on the market and may try to take advantage of a seller who has not been able to snag any fish on their hook.

Finally, it's a good idea to get a pest inspection done. It does not hurt to get a whole house and roof inspection too.

In your area, it may be mandatory to get a sewer inspection or something else that I have not thought of.

Also, if you were working with an agent, they would show you all the disclosures that need to be filled out.

Wherever you live, there will be mandatory disclosures. It's smart to have them filled out and ready for a buyer.

Chapter 3: Marketing

You know how much you want for your home. Now, you need to spread the word to everyone!

There are a group of people who are looking to own a home like yours, in your neighborhood at the price you are asking. These people are already driving around, looking for a "for sale" sign, searching the internet and going to open houses.

You may be thinking that "All I need is one good buyer," when you should be thinking that "All I need are two or three good buyers."

If one good buyer comes along, then you will negotiate something favorable to both of you. If two or three buyers want your home, then you call the shots.

You should find a good photographer to take some nice shots of the house. If you have a unique property and drone shots may enhance the visual experience, then pay a few hundred dollars. It can be worth it.

Get the photos and drone video online the day that you list your home for sale.
You can find a company who will get you on the MLS at a reasonable cost. Whatever you do, it's not a good idea to skimp on this cost.

If you are advertising on the MLS, then it's smart to offer a reasonable commission to agents who want to sell your home. Realize that you are competing with people who are usually offering 2.5 % to 3% to the buyer's agent (also referred to as the "selling agent").

There are people who offer a 1 %, 2% or flat fee also. If you offer a low fee to the selling agent, you may be ignored by a good chunk of agents; thus, not really saving any money.

When an agent sets up an MLS search for their client, they search price, area, square feet and they also can search for commissions that are no lower than a certain amount. Therefore, offering a little can cost you a lot.

You can ask your title company to get your labels so that you can send out postcards or letters to the neighbors.
You might say that "Why would my neighbors want to buy my house?"
You might send a mailer to people who are renting and cannot wait until the day they can move into their very own home in the neighborhood they love. These buyers are good because they are already sold on the location. They may work close by and have kids in a school close by.
Maybe these tenants are being told their rent is going up or maybe their landlord won't maintain the home. These buyers may look at you as a Godsend.

Knock on doors in the neighborhood. Plan an open house and print up some door hangers. Go to 100 houses around your house and talk to everyone you can. Leave a door hanger when no one is home.
When someone answers the door, simply invite them to your open house and give them a flyer.
90 % of them won't be interested but you can tell them that "This is your chance to pick your new neighbors" and ask if they know anyone who might want to move to the area.
If the neighbors own their own home, then it is in their best interest to see to it that you sell your home for top dollar.

The first sale I ever closed was a listing I had, where I knocked on doors for a week and I literally talked to 100 people.

A very nice woman introduced me to her twin nephews, and I helped them to buy their first home. This never would have happened if I did not get out and knock on doors. If you have the time, then this can be a very valuable experience.

In the past, open houses were not the best way to sell a home. But today, the open house is a very useful tool. Often times, the buyer finds the house before the real estate agent does. This is good for you as the buyers find your home on the internet, call you and ask for an appointment to see the house. Of course, you will also get a lot of calls from agents too, but you can use that to your advantage.

First of all, instead of showing the home to everyone who calls, it's a good idea to have an open house day set up. It's smart to tell the callers that they can come and see the home on Sunday from 1 to 4 or whatever time and day you schedule it.   This makes your life easier and it also compacts the showings into a short period of time, making everyone believe there is competition to buy the house and hopefully there is.

It is also a good idea to find a loan agent to sit at the open house with you to pre-qualify the buyers who are not already qualified.

So, you get a call from a prospective buyer, you should ask them:

Are you prequalified to buy in this price range? They will say "yes," "No" or "I have cash."

If the answer is yes, then ask who they are qualified with. If they tell you that "Suzie Jones and Red Diamond Loans on Market Street has qualified me for an FHA loan with 3.5 % down", then you know you are working with an educated buyer who is very serious.

The answer could be very different though. Sometimes you will get, "Well my bank qualified me a year ago and I'm sure I'm still qualified."

If you are making appointments to show your home, then you want to make sure that the buyers get their act together. This is why open houses are good.
You can ask this buyer to come to the open house from 1 to 4, not caring if they are wasting your time since you hopefully will have a nice parade of buyers coming through.

As the phone keeps ringing and real estate agents keep asking you to list with them, you can tell them that "No, but you are welcome to hold an open house for me and you will most likely get some great leads."
That agent might also knock on doors for you and may have a loan agent whom they can recommend to you.

Don't forget to use social media to advertise your open house. If you do this right, you should put in a good deal of time promoting the event, but if the home is priced right, they will come!

Chapter 4: The Transaction

Now you have been given an offer, or hopefully multiple offers.

This can be a wonderful experience or a frightening one.
If the buyers are represented by an agent, most likely the offer is written on a standard contract designed by the Association of Realtors ® in your state.

While these contracts are not the easiest to understand, they are far safer to use than a contract that the buyer has downloaded from some website.

Normally at this point, some sellers decide to pay an attorney to look over the offer. Warning! you want to hire an attorney who specializes in real estate in your state. You should not use the same lawyer who handled your divorce.

There was a time when I was new in the business. My client (the seller) had his attorney son-in-law look at the offer we received. The attorney obviously did not know much about our contracts and insisted on rewriting several paragraphs that really did not change much of anything.

Let's go over a few bullet points regarding the offer as we won't go into too much detail. Here, I list down certain things that you want to watch out at least.

#1 The price
   If you say yes to an offer, then the price is usually contingent on the appraisal.
   If you receive multiple offers, you may be able to get a buyer to wave that contingency or agree to pay up a certain dollar amount if the appraisal comes in low.

Be careful that you don't accept a ridiculously high offer from a buyer who "knows" the appraisal will come in low.

#2 Length of escrow

Typically, we see 30-day escrows. You need time to get out and your buyer needs time to get in. But maybe the home is already vacant, and you want it gone yesterday.

We closed a transaction not long ago with FHA loan in 11 days. If the buyer is approved by their lender or if the buyer has cash, a quick close can be very do-able.

If a buyer offers a quick close i.e. say 14 days, please talk to their lender and ask how realistic this is.

Get the buyer to pay a penalty, if they are late in closing like maybe $100 per day. All of a sudden that 14-day close may change to 21 or 30 days.

3 Type of financing

There may be no financing. Then you must see proof of funds. You should see a bank statement no more than 30 days old whereby you are given proof of liquid funds in the name of the buyer. Maybe the buyer is being given cash by his/her grandmother, then you will want to see a gift letter showing that their Grandma will transfer the money at the close of escrow.

VA Financing. If a veteran is buying, they can get 100 % financing up to a certain value and 75 % above that. For instance, if the VA will loan a veteran 100 % financing up to $500,000 in your area, then the buyer needs to put 25 % down for the amount above that up to a certain limit.

Today, the buyer cannot pay for the appraisal or a pest report on a VA loan. The seller must provide a current pest report with a section1 clearance. The lender can pay for the appraisal.

The appraiser will be stricter on a VA loan than an FHA or conventional. An FHA buyer will usually be coming with around 3.5% down. The pest report can be paid for by the buyer and it is not mandatory.

A conventional loan will have a considerably higher down payment and the guidelines for the appraisal are less strict.

Finally, there is what we call private money or "hard money " loan. These usually require a much higher down payment like 35%, the appraisal is not as strict, and it can close in a week. At this moment, it is my understanding that a buyer who plans on living in the home cannot use a private money loan. I believe that they are only for investors, but anything can change.

So, when you look at the offer, then of course cash is king, a hard money loan is very much like cash and a conventional loan is next in line. FHA and VA loans are less desirable.

Often times, someone with cash will offer you less than a VA buyer. You also might have a clear pest and you may not care when you close.

#4 The earnest money deposit (EMD)

You mostly may get people trying to take advantage of your perceived ignorance. They sometimes take those no-money-down classes where they learn that you can offer to put $100 down on a home.

Remember, no matter what the buyer is putting down to purchase the home, they are going to come out-of-pocket for closing costs. Therefore, I like to insist on at least a $5,000 deposit today. The money is refundable if the buyer backs out in the allotted time period.

#5 Time period for inspections

If you have provided inspection reports for the buyer, then you are ahead of the game. If the buyer is doing their own inspections which is very common, then 17 days is a fair time period. If there is a lot of competition, then some buyers will offer to conduct their inspections in a shorter period of time or may even wave that contingency immediately.

#6 The appraisal

If you give the buyer 17 days to get the home appraised and to remove that contingency, then they should be able to perform within that amount of time. The buyer may claim for an extension by giving an excuse that your property could be difficult to appraise. The key here is to make sure that the lender orders the appraisal on day one. If they do not, then you want to know why not. An appraisal that is not ordered right away is a big red flag, so get on top of this right away as there are no surprises 3 weeks from now.

#7 Re-negotiating

If the appraiser has written certain conditions into the appraisal or if it comes in low, you may be asked to abide. You'll never be told if the appraisal comes in high, only low. If it comes in low, insist on seeing the appraisal. If you are asked to fix a fence or a broken window because of the appraisal, you will have to do this if you want the financing to go through. Now, you may be able to ask the buyer to pay for it, but you usually can't get away with doing what needs to be done.

If the appraisal comes in low, it can be contested. Not long ago, an appraisal came in low and we asked the loan agent to contest it. She told me "In 17 years, I've never had an appraiser change their price." Well, we asked for it and the appraiser raised the value. So please, don't believe it when someone tells you something can't be done.

The buyer may present you with inspection reports and bids on work that needs to be done. Common responses are " This is not a new house," or "You already got a good deal" or "The work that needs to be done is already reflected in the price."

It's always fine to move at least a little towards what your buyer wants. If you can give the buyer credit towards closing costs, that is often times more desirable for both the buyer and seller.

#8 Back-up offers

If you had to say no to someone, it is nice to keep in touch with them just in case you need them if the first deal falls through. Reasons for a transaction falling apart can be a low appraisal, a lost job, a death etc.

I don't advise that you put someone in a back-up position because a better offer could very well come along once the first transaction falls apart.

#9 Final walk through

Your buyers are almost ready to close escrow. You were told that the buyer's docs are at the title company and ready for the buyer to sign. You go and sign your seller docs, and everything looks good.

The buyer now goes back to the house and walks through to make sure that everything is the way it was when they first looked at the house.

You want to keep all the utilities on until the end. Then the buyers' loan funds and the deed are recorded at the recorder's office. Once you are told by the title company or escrow officer that the deed has been recorded, you can expect the escrow company to either issue you a check or they may wire your funds.

If you get an email from the title company asking for your bank account, do not respond via email as this is a potential scam. Pick up the phone and talk to the escrow officer or more than likely you will have filled out a form already in person, authorizing the proceeds to be wired to your account.

When escrow closes, then you and all of your belongings must be moved out of the home. The contract may say that you have until 6 P.M. that night or it may say you need to be out at 10 A.M. that day. When in doubt, read the contract.

#10 Sign out

Take down your "For Sale" sign and remove any info about the home being available off the internet as you probably don't want any more phone calls.

At this time, you will either be very happy with yourself or you may say "I'll never do this again."

Congratulations, you have just sold your home. Hopefully, you received as much or more than the other similar homes in the neighborhood.

Chapter 5: What Could Go Wrong?

So far, I have outlined the typical scenarios. But what happens when things go wrong?

Here are a few things that can go wrong:

1. The earnest money deposit is late:
   On the typical contract, your buyer has 72 hours to place their deposit in escrow. You want to try and use the escrow company you have built a reputation with, but if the buyer is paying their own title and escrow fees then you cannot force them to use your company.

   Typically, you want to be able to ask the escrow company to give you a receipt for the deposit the minute it arrives, and you want to be able to get a hold of them quickly if you have any questions.

   You don't want to work with a company that puts you on hold or sends you to voice mail every time you call. If you find out the money is not in escrow, you need to give notice to the buyer that you can and will kill the deal if the deposit does not arrive in the next 48 hours.

2. Assignable contracts:
   You want to work with a contract that the buyer cannot assign to another buyer. Make sure that no part of the contract says that it is assignable.

   There are "buyers" who will tie up your property and then try to sell the contract to another buyer. If they cannot sell the contract, they will back out at the last minute. Two signs that this is the goal are one, a very low deposit and two, the contract is not a standard contract, but one pulled off some website or purchased through a seminar.

3. Lease option:
   It is where a buyer purchases an option from you to buy the house at some later date at a predetermined price. You might put your home on the

market in the summer and someone might talk you into selling them the option to buy the home by Christmas.

You are happy because the buyer pays you to rent for a few months while they work on saving up the down payment or raising their credit score. You really don't need to sell until the end of the year and the buyer is willing to pay you more than you were asking.

The problem is that 90 % of lease options never are exercised and when December rolls around, you just might be trying to evict someone.

4. House of cards:

If you are selling your house to buy another home and your buyer is doing the same, then if one deal falls through, then everyone loses out. The better idea is for you not to make an offer on another home until your buyer has removed all of their contingencies. In this scenario, it is smart to have arranged to be able to rent the back your own home at the close of escrow. The amount of rent is usually the same as your buyer's PITI (Principle, interest, taxes, and insurance.)

5. Early move-in:

Your buyer explains that there is a delay with their close of escrow and they will pay you to rent if you just let them move in a few days early.

You say "yes" and all of a sudden, the buyer needs another month because they decided to change lenders. Then, you hear excuse after excuse, and you realize you are being cheated.

It is always best to let the buyers not move in early, even if they make you feel bad about them being kicked out of their apartment.

6. Lawsuits that hold up the close of escrow:

Recently we served buyers who used their VA loan to buy a home that had been owned by an LLC that had bought, fixed and flipped a house. The sellers dragged their feet, getting the pest clearance and in the meantime got sued and were not allowed to sell the house. Fortunately for us, the seller did not read #5 above. The seller allowed my buyers to move into the house early, paying no rent. The simple little court issue dragged out for 2 months, allowing the buyers not to make payments for 60 days.

So, the moral of that story is that if the sellers got the pest work cleared in a timely manner, they could have sold the home before the judge told them not to. Doubtlessly, a lot of heartaches would have been avoided.

7. Buyer's remorse or shot gunning:

A buyer may all of a sudden decide they don't want your house for a myriad of reasons, but your goal should be to guard against buyer's remorse and shot gunning by keeping your eyes open.

If a buyer is on the fence or he/she is making out offers on a hand-full of homes at the same time, you can get them to show how serious you are day one by insisting on a big enough deposit. I like $5,000.

By ensuring that the appraisal is ordered right away, and the deposit is placed in escrow quickly, then you will know if the buyers are serious. In situations where buyers do not perform quickly; if you are on top of them, then you can insist through written notices to perform and get off the pot before they waste too much of your time.

8. Troubleshoot with loan officer:

Finally, we recently experienced a transaction where the loan officer actually went into rehab while the transaction was in escrow because we asked about the appraisal every day, things did not drag out too long. In other words, the loan agent can screw up the deal, so if you see this happening, ensure that the loan officer is replaced so you don't have to replace the buyer.

9. Tax issues:

You may find out too late that there is a tax lien against you that you did not know about. This is another reason why you want to get the title company to pull a property profile on day one. There also could be a mechanic's lien or something else you did not know about. You don't want a buyer who must move soon to back out of a deal because they don't want you to resolve your IRS tax issue or some other similar problem.

"If you do not like real estate, all you have to do is make hamburgers, build a business around that hamburger, and franchise it."
Robert Kiyosaki

Section 2: If You Change Your Mind

Hopefully, now you either have the confidence to sell your own home or maybe you have tried it for a week or two and have decided that maybe it's not for you.

If you have thought about the money aspect, you probably have learned that there is a huge chance that working without an agent in your corner will probably cost you more than it will save you.
Not convinced? Let's do the math:

You want to sell your $400,000 house. You don't like the idea of paying a $24,000 commission.
You put it on the market, and you get an offer for $376,000 from a buyer who realizes you are not using an agent, so they write in their own 6 % discount.

You decide to offer a 3 % commission to a buyer's agent, so now you get a $400,000 offer, you are paying $12,000 commission, bravo, but 3 weeks into the transaction the buyers ask for a closing cost credit of $6,000 and they insist you replace a deck at the cost of $6,000. They have a pest report that would be very costly to clear and if you get rid of the clients you know that you must disclose the report to any future buyers.

In addition, you never had many qualified buyers show up, so you are thinking that you probably could have sold for $415,000 if you had more exposure. At the end of the day, you realize that you did not save a dime. You are wishing you could turn back time and hire an agent day 1!

"Working with the Meyer Team, not only do you get the vast experience that Jim and his team bring to the table, you get a great negotiator working on your behalf who has a knack for sprinkling in a great sense of humor to break-up the sometimes, tense and nerve-racking moments that buying or selling may bring. Altogether, you have honest, hardworking people, who love what they do, and know how to close the deal."
Joey Lafon

Chapter 1: Choosing A Good Agent

It's good to interview several prospective agents before taking a final decision.

You should ask them how they would price your home, how they would market it, how long it might take to sell it and how much money you will put in your pockets at the close of escrow?

Be careful not just hire the person who brags about being #1.

I made the mistake when selling two condos that I owned out of the area. I thought that choosing a "top producer" would guarantee success.

When it came time to close, my "top producer" agent disappeared and I had to deal directly with the buyer's agent.

My advice is to make sure that the agent you work with is a full-time agent with no other job, or that they are teamed up with someone else who fills in the gaps that they leave.

Knowledge can be learned but it's tough to fake enthusiasm and hunger.

You should be working with an agent who is hungry to serve you and get you top dollar in an ethical and honest manner.

You should be working with someone who loves to learn, to grow and to please you.

Even if the agent is not full of experience, as long as they are connected to people who will make sure they do everything correctly and that your best interests are forefront, then you should be OK.

"The Meyer Team is diligent and enthusiastic, and an absolute pleasure to work with"
Kelly Guglielmo

Chapter 2: Jim Meyer and the Meyer Team

What is the Meyer team? Well, it's more than just a hand-full of Realtors ® who work full time with your best interests in mind.

We also have a transaction coordinator who makes sure that you fill out and sign all the up-to-date disclosures for the sale of your home and that the buyer does the same in a timely manner. There are different regional disclosures that she is familiar with. So, wherever you are, we provide you with the correct disclosures.

We work with escrow officers who are experts at keeping on top of each transaction. An escrow officer who is not on top of their game can harm a transaction in big or small ways. Just getting something done a day late could mean you closing your transaction on a Monday instead of that Friday you were hoping for.

The title companies we work with also help us to market your home in ways described earlier and I'd love to go over this in more detail with you.

We work closely with loan officers who are available early in the morning, on weekends and late at night to do what has to be done to close transactions that lazy lenders might not be able to.

"I was a first-time home buyer and had no idea what was all evolved with purchasing a house. The Jim Meyer team really helped me translate and negotiate what I wanted from seller and also call me on something that may sound "stupid" (my words not his, well maybe) if I/we asked for that specific thing, but while still rephrasing it to get some wiggle room and a better deal. So, having master negotiator and deal-maker while purchasing a house was so helpful than my trying to figure it out myself."
Kyle Starr

"I highly recommend the Meyer team. Very informative and listen to what you're looking for. They truly know the market. I closed in 30 days of working with them."
Martha Hunter

Chapter 3: What To Expect From Us

We would hope that you have high expectations from us as you can choose to work with anyone, and we'd like to earn your business.

We will work with you to price your home for sale with the goal of selling for top dollar and in a timely manner. We will never tell you what to do, but we will tell you our honest opinion.

When we market your property; we are contacted via e-mail, text, and phone.
We pride ourselves on the ability to respond to inquiries fast and many times instantly.

A lot of times, we sell to out-of-area buyers who are working with Realtors ® who cannot access our lockboxes. We have ways of accommodating these agents.

When it's time to let the appraiser in, we like to be there with comps. We like to feel out the situation with the appraiser when they inspect the property, letting you know immediately if there should be a concern.

While some agents will tell you that open houses are a waste of time, we have proven to ourselves how valuable they can be for the number of reasons.

We also make hundreds of cold phone calls every week to invite people to come to your open house and to spread the word to their friends, asking if they would like to "pick their new neighbors."

Once an offer or offers come in, we like to make the buyers compete for the right to buy your home, hopefully for more than asking price. We like to create a sense of urgency to get you a buyer who will close as fast as possible with few demands.

As problems arise, we have seen most everything and can handle them allowing you to go about your business, knowing that we are putting out fires and working behind the scenes to ensure your peace of mind.

I met Jim Meyer in 1995, I was so amazed at his energy and dedication to taking personal care of his Clients. His work ethic has remained the same over all these years!
Brenda Jones Placer Title Company

Chapter 4: How To Get Started With Us

First off, thank you for allowing us to serve you.

Once you have decided how you want to price your home, we can write up the listing agreement.

We can meet in person for signatures or we can digitally sign the agreement.
If there are multiple owners such as husband and wife, we need each of you to have different e-mail addresses.

We will also inform via e-mail or bring you some disclosures that must be filled in with a pen. Some can just be digitally signed.

It's smart for us to order a pest inspection right away. You should make sure nothing is obstructing the view of the inspector as he/she examines walls and crawl spaces.

We would like to put up our MLS lockbox for showings. When an agent shows the home, we get a notification as to who and when they showed the home.

We can ask that the home only be shown at certain times or by appointment only.

We like to take professional photos and maybe even do a drone video.

The "For Sale" sign with our phone number is very important. We do not like putting up a flyer box as we want people to call us directly for the price.

 At this point, you probably have a few questions so feel free to contact us any time.

Thank you very much for reading the whole book. It means a lot to us!

Jim is smart, kind & considerate. He listens well & has his client's interests at heart. If you want to sell or trade buy real estate, he's your man!
Sue Goodrich Greenday Power

We have been working with The Meyer Team for many years and they know how to get the job done for you. No matter your circumstance they will remain committed to helping you.
Doug Pyne & Kristi Jones
Caliber Home Loans

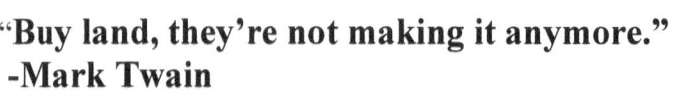

"Buy land, they're not making it anymore."
-Mark Twain

Glossary

Acceptance

When there is a meeting of the minds between buyer and seller and the offer or counteroffer is signed by both parties and delivered to both parties.

Agreement

The contract that includes the offer of all counters and addenda signed by all parties.

C.A.R. Form

Real estate contractual forms written by the California Association of Realtors.

Close Of Escrow (COE)

The date that ownership is transferred to the buyer and the deed is recorded.

Contingencies

A purchase contract will usually stipulate that the sale is contingent on certain contingencies. The most common are inspection, loan, appraisal, sale of another property and title search.

Counteroffer

An offer is made. If not rejected, it is countered. There can be numerous backs and forth counters but once the initial terms are agreed to; then there are no more counteroffers. During the escrow period, the price and terms can be re-negotiated with addendums, repair requests, and extensions.

Days

The contract refers to calendar days. COE will not occur on a weekend or holiday.

Days After

Refers to the number of calendar days after a specific event ending at 11:59 PM.

Days Prior

A specified number of calendar days before an event.

Deed and Title

The title is a document that proves you own a property. The deed is the legal document that facilitates the transfer of deeds from one party to another.

Deliver, Delivered or Delivery

Transfer of possession of a real or personal property from one person to another.

Disclosure

Sellers must disclose known property defects. There are many disclosure forms that aid in the delivery of such information. An owner should not confuse as-is with permission to not disclose.

Down Payment

This can be anywhere from nothing down with a VA loan to 20 % or more with a conventional loan.

Generally, the more you put down the better the interest rate and less likely the chance you will have to pay a mortgage insurance premium.

In addition to the down payment, buyers will have to come up with closing costs which they need to factor into their total out-of-pocket buying expenses.

Earnest Money Deposit (EMD)

This is the money that a buyer puts in escrow to secure a property as they go through their purchase. The money is refundable up until the contingencies are all removed.

"Electronic Copy" or "Electronic Signature"

It means an applicable electronic copy or signature complying with California Law.

Buyer and Seller agree that electronic means will not be used by either Party to modify or alter the content or integrity of this Agreement without the knowledge and consent of the other Party.

Escrow

Escrow is an arrangement where a neutral third party facilitates the transaction, taking in a deposit, transferring money from buyer to seller and managing the transaction.

Extension

If a buyer needs more time to obtain an appraisal, complete inspections or get their finances in order, it is common to ask for an extension. Sellers weigh the facts and often benefit by giving a buyer a little more time.

Federal Housing Administration (FHA)

The FHA ensures mortgage insurance; so that qualified buyers can purchase homes with as little as 3.5 % down.

Good-Faith Estimate (GFE) or Closing Disclosure

This is a detailed itemization of all the costs associated with the financing of a home, provided by the lender to the borrower

HOA (Homeowner's Association)

Condo complexes will collect a monthly fee to maintain the common areas etc. Certain detached home subdivisions have HOA's too. Make sure that you know what the HOA covers and what it costs before you make an offer.

Home Equity

Equity is the difference between what you owe on your home and what it is worth today.

Home Inspection

Of all the money a buyer spends, this is probably the best dollar for dollar investment. A good inspector will take their time and point out any deficiency the home has to the buyer, explaining if the problems found are major or minor. The inspector will provide a written report with pictures that the buyer can use to re-negotiate the price, ask for repairs or a closing cost credit.

Home Warranty

This is an annual service contract that covers appliance and systems in the home. Often times, a seller or agent will spend the $400 which can be well worth it.

Law

It means any law, code, statute, ordinance, regulation, rule or order, which is adopted by a controlling city, county, state or

Federal

Legislative, judicial or executive body or agency.

Lien

When a party says they are owed a debt by the owner of the property, they can place a lien on it. There are both voluntary and involuntary liens. A buyer and seller should find out what liens are attached to the property very early in the transaction.

Listing

An agreement that a property owner and a broker enter into whereby the owner contracts with the broker for a specific period of time to sell the property for a commission or fee.

Loan Originator

A loan originator will qualify a borrower and find a loan product that suits them. Then, the LO will serve the client as they borrow money from a lender to purchase or refinance their home.

Multiple Listing Service (MLS)

There are roughly 900 MLS's in the US. Agents load a listing onto the service and share it with other agents in specific service areas. Much of the information is not public, such as commission, owner and tenant phone numbers and alarm codes. Much of the information is public such as the asking price, home size and open house times. This public information is usually shared on all the major websites such as Realtor.Com, Trulia and Zillow.

Pre-Approval and Pre-Qualification

Pre-qualification gives you an idea of what a buyer can afford.

Pre-approval is the next step means that a borrower has submitted their documentation and is conditionally approved to borrow up to a certain dollar amount.

Principal, Interest, Taxes, and Insurance (PITI)

When figuring out what you need to pay monthly for your home, always ask your loan officer "What is my PITI?" Add the HOA payment too if you have an HOA.

REALTOR®

REALTOR® is a federally registered collective membership mark which identifies a real estate professional who is a member of the NATIONAL ASSOCIATION OF REALTORS® and subscribes to its strict Code of Ethics.

Signed

Signed means that a party to the transaction has hand-signed or digitally signed the contract, a copy of the contract or any counterpart of the contract.

Short Sale

When a homeowner wishes to sell but owes more than the home is worth, they can apply to sell their home "short" of what is owed. These transactions can take a lot of time to get approved, but once sold, the seller has avoided foreclosure on their record.

Title Insurance

Numerous potential title defects can arise. Both buyers and lenders obtain title insurance for this reason.

VA Loan

The Department of Veteran Affairs (VA) offers special mortgages to members of the US military. There are specific rules in regard to what kind of property can be purchased.

Walkthrough

You are almost ready to close escrow. The buyer walks through the property making sure all is as it should be. It is too late for the buyer to make any new demands unless they discover that something about the property has changed.

Examples: Ceiling fans have been replaced with cheaper ceiling fans, a tree has fallen on the roof or a carpet has been torn out.

Client Review

"I am a former client of Jim Meyer's, and now a good friend. I bought my home in World Marine in American Canyon in 2015. I was driving through the park and saw a couple of for sale signs.

The first Realtor did not even bother to call me back, but Jim did. We met up the next day and he showed me a house that did not even have a for sale sign posted.

I ended up making an offer the next day. Jim was so easy to work with, not at all pushy but a very relaxed man. He really was very easy to deal with, letting me in at various times so I could take measurements, etc.

Mind you, it is not easy for him to get around, but he did not let that stop him. The Realtor that had the listing was not very accommodating and after a few calls to her, he told her to Do Your Job.

He managed to get me a few extra deals on the home even though it was sold as-is. The fences were in horrid conditions and he wrote it up in the contract to be replaced, which they were.

I would definitely give him the sale of my home if I were going to list it (which I am not) but who knows what the future holds.

Jim Meyer is honest, dependable, hardworking, always there for you, definitely calls you back and I truly make friends with the majority of his clients. So, feel assured you will be in good hands with his team whether buying or selling your home.

Out of a score of 10, I would give him a 12 and he also has open houses, whatever it takes to get it sold!"

Jamie Schwafel.

Author's Contact Information

For more information, feel free to contact us at any time.

Jim Meyer
Broker Associate
License # 01036142
RE/MAX Gold Meyer team
MeyerJames@Aol.Com
707-580-5391
707-580-5393
www.facebook.com/JamesEricMeyer
https://www.pinterest.com/remaxgoldmeyerteam/

www.ingramcontent.com/pod-product-compliance
Lightning Source LLC
Chambersburg PA
CBHW021048180526
45163CB00005B/2334